On Woodworking

Notes From a Lifetime at the Bench

Zachary J. Dillinger

Also By Zachary J. Dillinger

With Saw, Plane and Chisel: Building Historic American Furniture with Hand Tools

First Edition

ISBN:
978-1986351188

Zachary J. Dillinger

To those who ask unanswerable questions in
a world of unquestioned answers

CONTENTS

ACKNOWLEDGMENTS

First, my wife April and my daughter Abigail, without whom I would never have made the leap into writing. Next, my mother Judi and her husband Mike and April's parents Terry and Debra, who all have supported me non-stop and also provided countless hours of free babysitting. Finally, my friends and fellow woodworkers who have helped me learn and do so much in our shared craft.

INTRODUCTION

For the better part of the last three decades, I have been obsessed with building things. I don't know why the obsession exists, though I suspect it has something to with my supernaturally strong drive to understand the universe around me. Whatever the reason for my obsession, it has turned out to be one of the most rewarding elements of my life. I've gotten to meet interesting people, see amazing things, and visit incredible places simply because I have been able to build some beautiful things and, in all honesty, a few not so beautiful things.

The same drive to first understand and then build the things that fascinate me has led to this, my second book. Throughout my woodworking life I have sought to understand why the craftsman of the past made the choices they did, why certain pieces survived while others failed or were discarded, and the thought processes of my fellow craftsman with regards to the work and hobby for which we share a passion. Consequently, I am an inveterate note taker, constantly writing down thoughts, quips, quotes, and ideas whenever they come to me. It is this lifetime of notes that has served as the source from which this book is drawn.

The book, much like my shop, is loosely organized into categories. While my shop has tool chests, racks, and shelves to hold my planes, chisels, and saws, this book has sections about tools, materials the process, the furniture itself, history and the people who actually get the work done as well as those who just talk about it. My thoughts range in length from single words to entire essays. If you have read my blog, my articles, or my previous book With Saw, Plane and Chisel, some of the themes will be familiar to you. I happen to believe in the political idea that people will only start to believe a given idea if they hear it seven or more times. Some of these ideas are beginning to approach that level of exposure. For those of you who already agree with me on these topics, welcome to the club.

My goal with this collection of musings is simply to make you think about what we do and how we do it. You will find no projects, no measured drawings, and no ideas for things to make. I usually tell people that I consider myself more of an experimental archaeologist than a furniture maker; in this work I indulge in my delusions that I am something of a practical philosopher. I hope that some of it makes sense to you.

In short, you might think of this book as transcript of a conversation that might have been overhead in a bar between two woodworkers sometime in the past. There's a bit of poetry, a bit of ribaldry, a bit of philosophy, and a little bit of practical advice. If you get nothing else from this book, I hope you get a laugh or two.

A quick word about the photography selected. I must say that being able to choose pictures for their artistic merit, rather than their ability to convey a step in a process, is incredibly freeing.

A beautiful pair of 18th century dividers

ON TOOLS

A woodworking haiku:

Sawplate sharp and set
Teeth cut swiftly through the pine
Blast! It's still too short!

The best tools in the world in the unskilled hands of the amateur are fully capable of producing the best and highest quality work but only by sheer accident. Always remember that 90% of the shot comes from the archer, not the arrow: the arrow can only go where the archer tells it to go. Set a target and try to hit it. The tools can certainly hinder you on that path but, ideally, they will simply allow you to express in reality what previously has only existed in your mind.

I use hand tools. I eschew the use of power tools at every turn, even for something as simple as drilling a pilot hole. I hate the clouds of dust thrown up by sanders and power saws. I hate the noise of universal motors. I hate the danger that is ever present when carbide teeth are spinning at a high rate of speed. All of these things can be mitigated with proper safety equipment and clothing but I work wood to enjoy myself, not to be suited up like a diver on an extended deep sea expedition. I wouldn't recommend this to anyone but I often work barefoot.

But I do what I do for a more profound reason than simple comfort. I do what I do because that is how it was done 250 years ago. In my hobby work (the things I make for me), I try to replicate 18th c. style pieces as closely as my skills allow. This means doing the work with the "proper" tools. I'm not judging power tools as "improper" in every case, but they are improper for the work I enjoy, where period accuracy is desired above all else.

18th century woodwork is full of what we would today term "flaws". Surfaces, even show surfaces, show tearout. Boards are thicknessed unevenly. Sometimes the marks from the saw pit or the tell-tale marks of riving are left untouched. Boards cup and tear out hinges because the original builder didn't take into account seasonal movement, at least to the extent we would consider necessary. Drawer runners get nailed on to case sides across the grain, what many would consider a major structural flaw.

It's more than just surface quality. Designing and building with hand tools, when properly done, yields a piece that looks handmade because of the overall composition of these "flaws" and design decisions based on the existing material specifications. You don't design a piece to an exact dimension, you make it work with the wood you have. You don't plane 7/8 down to 3/4, just because this is the dimension you see in the plan, you make 7/8 work.

This cannot be done with power tools, no matter if you have the latest Nurffurr 5000 variably-spaced dovetail jig. Those machine cut joints stand out like sore thumbs. So do router-made moldings. They are too perfect and look terrible on period work.

Taking walnut shavings with a finely set try plane

Since my goal is to make things look as much like the original as possible, I do not worry about the modern definition of "flaw". Sure, my surfaces sometimes show a little tearout, which usually goes away, visually, under shellac. My turnings are not identical and often show tool marks from my skew. My moldings show a little "movement" and are not identical from one foot to the next. My boards aren't perfectly flat (not hard to see why, my straightedge is Stick-of-Cherry, not Starrett). They are wavy, undulating, tactile, warm surfaces that show the pieces was made by hand, something that a machine cannot do. They are just flat enough to do what I need them to do. No more, no less.

That is why I use hand tools. In no way should anything I ever say, anywhere, be taken to mean that I hate power tools, or that I somehow consider power tool work as less than hand tool work. It is just different. If my goal were different, I might very well put on the apron, safety glasses, hearing protection and fire up a Sawstop or a lunch-box planer.

Tools are nothing more than a means to an end. If you can achieve your goals with power tools, than "more power" to you. Some of us have goals that cannot be met if we use power tools so we don't use them. Most people have a goal that allows them to use both, so they use both. There isn't a merit badge for ripping with a handsaw, and there isn't a

PETA campaign (of which I am aware) to "Save the Electrons".

A means to an end. Nothing more, and nothing less. That is what makes them so incredible.

A 19th century Scottish infill jointer plane

If you like hand tools use them. If you don't, don't use them. If you don't know what you like, try many different tools, techniques, and processes. Give anything and everything a fair shake. I used table saws, planers, and bandsaws for a decade or more before I finally grew sick of them.

Many people decry hand tools as 'too slow'. A person using hand tools can produce a piece of furniture just as fast, if not faster, than a person using power tools provided that the wielder of the hand tools thinks the appropriate way. There is no virtually no need to foursquare boards for the hand tool woodworker, we just make a reference edge and face before making the other side look "good enough". We don't have to make test cut after test cut to set up a router table; we grab a molding plane with the shape coded in and go to town. If your try plane is appropriately sharp and set up properly, you don't have to smooth plane the entire case side down when you get a little tearout; whereas you must with a machine planed surface. It's the little things like that that make a difference.

This is, of course, predicated on the idea of making one-offs; in a production world it is obviously far less expensive to automate and electrify the work provided the design lends itself to this type of work. Since most of us are not doing woodwork on an industrial scale, it is just as fast. I'll put it this way; my William and Mary spice chest, the first piece for which I was truly recognized by the larger woodworking world, took me less than 90 hours from rough wood to finished product. The Hepplewhite huntboard from my book *With Saw, Plane and Chisel* was about 20 hours of work. The footstool features cabriole legs which can be done by hand in less than one hour each (not including the foot). I'd lay a friendly challenge at the feet of any power tool person to execute those designs that fast to an appropriate level of period accuracy.

In my world, speed is but one consideration and I would argue it isn't even the most important. Fidelity to the past is what matters to me. Replicating a piece of furniture means more than just copying shapes from a photograph and putting on a mirror-like finish. Workmen of the past did not engage in their craft as a worthwhile and enjoyable hobby as most do today; they were simply trying to earn a living so that they might feed themselves, their families, and perhaps save a little for the future. This led them to work quickly and to a salable level.

I try to accomplish the same thing in my shop; work quickly and to the level of finish I see on the piece I have chosen to replicate. This often means violating today's aesthetic sensibilities and leaving things behind that show the process... why this isn't acceptable in modern work I'll never understand.

When we work to a pre-industrial standard we free ourselves from the modern idea of perfection and we can gain a bit of appreciation for what it must have been like for the craftsman who came before. I often say I consider myself an experimental archaeologist more than a furniture maker; I want to experience everything I can with regard to the life of past craftsman. This means clothing, lighting, temperature (my shop is unheated for example), everything I can reasonably do. I'll keep my modern medicine though, thank you very much.

The view behind my workbench

Few things annoy me more than an antique store that sells antique hand tools as 'primitives'. There is nothing primitive about them and only the truly uneducated think otherwise. I would pity them for their ignorance if they didn't try to charge me three times what something is worth just because they can write that particular word on the price tag. And don't get me started on the 'repurposing' trend. If I see one more wooden plane ruined and wired into a lamp or another painted saw, I may just lose my mind.

Primitive? I think not... photo of tools taken at Jamestown Settlement

Sure, you want that new tool but do you need it? You should probably only buy things you absolutely need… oh, who am I kidding… wanting a tool is a more than good enough reason to buy it as long as you can still make rent or your mortgage payment and feed yourself. If not, I suggest buying a Lie-Nielsen #8 jointer plane… they come in boxes almost big enough to live in. Life is too damn short to deny yourself the simple pleasures of opening such a box.

Without question, I buy more saws, planes and chisels than I need. I justify it by saying that, someday, I might use up my planes and will need others. That is a lame excuse of course but, hey, it could happen. I think the real reason for a lot of guys belongs in a Highlander-like movie. There can only be one and until they have tried every available option, they will never know what that 'one' is.

That said, I think it is important to focus on improving skills rather than buying the latest and greatest tools and technology I do this because my goal is to make furniture not build a shop. Many see building a shop or buying tools as a hobby unto itself. Too many hobby woodworkers think like factory workers and try to "improve" the process by introducing new tools and jigs to replace the essential manual skills. I try to think like a pre-industrial woodworker who gets the job done and moves on to the next piece. This is actually driven by a profound hatred of repetition and the fact that I am easily bored. One of the selling points of my furniture is exclusivity; no two pieces are exactly alike. Although this is a great line, the fact is I can't stand to do the same thing twice and, even if I could, hand tools ensure that nothing is ever identical.

We get paralysis by analysis fed to us on a daily basis. We think we have to be perfectly tooled up to make even a simple table. We see endless commentary about sharpening methods and how flat your sole must be to make your plane work (despite many craftsman who don't worry about such trivialities). All of this leads to confusion, to buying, and to not building anything. That is no darn good! So all that said, I'm always in favor of action instead of analysis so if buying a dovetail jig will get you in the shop making stuff that is all that matters.

My 15 year old, recently retired bench hook

Fast, good, or cheap. Pick any two. This idea applies to many areas of life but nowhere is it more accurate than in choosing tools for woodworking. The inexpensive saw on the shelf at the hardware store isn't going to be good without significant work to tune it. The premium hand plane that is just a phone call or mouse click away isn't going to be cheap. The hunt for the well-used and well-loved vintage chisels isn't going to be quick. It's up to you to prioritize and decide what matters most to you.

Always remember that you're buying the tool, not emotional attachment. Keep in mind that a seller's story is usually nothing more than a story, and never pay over the odds just because that chisel allegedly belonged to his 'blind cousin twice removed who once build a cabinet for the Queen". These stories are, to a one, total bullshit. Don't be a sucker and buy into them.

The topic of buying vintage or new tools is an interesting one to me. There are vintage tools of superb quality that surpass most of what is available today. There are new tools made today that far exceed the quality of virtually every other tool ever made. The question, to me anyway, is how much of this "quality" is actually needed to make furniture. Up to a certain quality point, the tool itself can hinder the execution of the work (this point is "lower" for a skilled tradesman who can make the most out of junk if forced to do so).

Beyond this point, the quality of the tool adds very little to the actual execution of the work (perhaps speed and efficiency but, again, a skilled tradesman will be able to work quickly with just about anything of passable quality). After this, using the higher quality tool is purely for the enjoyment of the user. Not something typically associated with a professional, who must make each dollar spent on tooling count to the utmost.

Take my planes, for example. I have a "complete" set of infills (I lack an infill miter and good rebate plane, but I'm in the market if you have some for sale), literally hundreds of vintage wooden planes, and a couple of LN planes. I usually work with nothing but the vintage wooden planes, even if they aren't of the same "high quality" that the other planes are. They work well enough to execute my designs. Anything beyond that is purely for my own gratification and doesn't actually affect my ability to do my work.

A few planes from my infill collection

I use a chunk of paraffin wax to lubricate the soles of all my planes while in use. This accomplishes four tasks, all for less than a nickel's worth of paraffin. While rubbing the wax onto the sole, simply pass it over at both corners of the mouth and in the middle. This checks the lateral adjustment of the iron and also gives me a pretty good idea of the shaving thickness the plane is likely to produce. It lubricates the interior surfaces of the mouth opening which can help the plane eject shavings cleanly and avoids the dreaded clumping that is common in planes. It also accomplishes the primary intent of lubricating the sole of the plane which makes the work of planing less difficult. Four benefits in one and all for just a couple dollars for a lifetime supply. Hard to beat that.

You can muddle through a job with half-sharp tools, but sooner or later a dull-ish tool will negatively impact your work, or your finger, as you try to force the tool to do work for which it is not prepared. It takes more force and more effort to do the job. Dull tool plus increased force equals ruined work and copious amounts of blood. No exceptions. Don't tempt fate, sharpen your tools regularly.

This is the only thing I have to say about choosing a sharpening system. There are at least half a dozen or more good options out there. Pick one. Stick with it. Learn it. Don't obsess over the relative merits of one system or the other or get stuck in 'paralysis by analysis', a sure way to get nothing done. Any one of the available systems will do the job adequately if you get your mind out of the way and just learn how it works.

For the record I use vintage oil stones, including a lovely translucent Arkansas stone I bought from the grandson of a long-dead patternmaker. On those stones I use Marvel Mystery Oil and I wipe away the swarf and oil after each use. I finish on a strop loaded with Noxon metal polish. My entire current setup costs me less than $30.

I speculate that most of what artisans of the past knew about getting sharp tools was taught to them by the person who taught them the trade, i.e. "you will use this stone in this manner at this time to sharpen tools while you work for me". They weren't bombarded by 74 different systems, techniques, and teachers. There is a lesson to learn there.

My sharpening setup

I use a $0.97 cinder block from Lowes to flatten my oil stones when I buy them. I have never found it necessary to flatten them again after I've performed the initial correction. This is due to a technique that I learned firsthand from an old master. When you sharpen freehand, you can make a conscious 'Figure 8' while honing the bevel. Use every square inch of the stone while doing this. When you are removing the wire edge from the tool, again use every inch of the stone. If you can stop yourself from working only in one area of the stone and can spread the wear out over the entire surface, you won't wear the stone unevenly. Easy peasy.

A fine reproduction of a rare 18th century saw

Moving fillister plane in use

A fine paring cut in end grain pine

The wooden plow plane is truly the workhorse joinery plane of the hand tool or hybrid shop. It cuts grooves for a panel door faster than you can set up a router table. It can be used to cut rabbets by burying the iron in the plane fence, rather like setting up a sacrificial fence on a table saw. It can be used to mark out, and even begin a long and accurate rip saw cut, whether you make the cut by hand or band saw. Even if you aren't committed to working entirely by hand, a vintage wooden plow can be a great fit for your shop and a complement to your power tools. I highly recommend that you get one and try it out. It may end up being a bit of an obsession with you like it has me. I have bought more plows than just about any other kind of plane, and have also made several of my own. A good plow is highly enjoyable to use.

It is good practice to lay out your grooves with a marking gauge before using your plow. The purpose is to ensure you plow a straight groove, as fences on plows do slip and the lines let you see if / when that happens. Severing the grain in less-friendly wood is a happy by-product of this effort. Plowing with the grain usually works just fine without tearing things up anyway.

When using a fenced plane, such as a plow or a moving fillister, it is important that you use each hand appropriately to produce square work. Your left hand must only push the fence of the tool tightly to the reference edge; your right hand must only push the tool forward and into the cut. Do not attempt to steer the plane with your right hand or to push the plane forward with your left. This is bad technique and your work will be the worse for it.

A walnut plow plane I made in my shop

Using a sash fillister plane

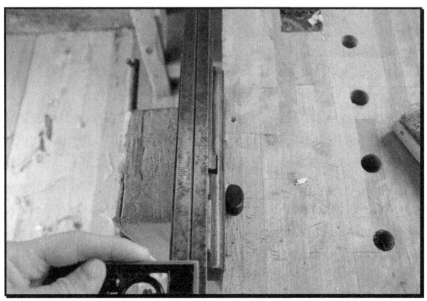

Checking a plow plane's skate for square

Four plow planes from my collection

I don't think it matters how you put your planes down on your bench if you work in a dedicated woodshop. I prefer to place them sole down to make sure I don't bash the iron with a holdfast or accidentally run my hand into the sharp edge. I know that other people are taught differently. I do not understand why people argue about this. Do whatever you want, it's your tool, your bench, and your thumb. I'm not the one who is going to stitch the wound or clean the blood off your bench when you cut yourself.

Shooting end grain with a large wooden jointer plane

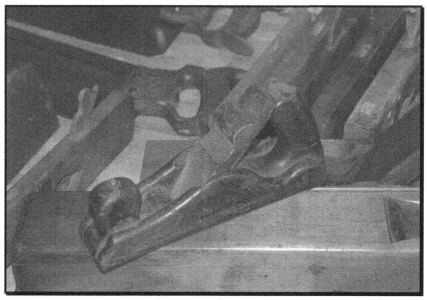

An interesting Marples smoothing plane

You see 18th century American planes with offset totes. I made my "non-throwaway"30" maple jointer with an offset tote and I like it. I can't swear to what it does, ergonomics wise, but I imagine that the guys who were pushing them for large portions of their lives had a reason for it. I suppose it does provide an interesting balancing force to the force that one applies essentially to left side of the toe of the plane when pushing down with the left hand. This could rotate the plane slightly and perhaps the offset tote provides the opposite force to level out the sole in relation to the wood. This is something a skilled plane user does instinctively anyway, so who knows. Either way, it looks cool.

With regards to shooting planes, I believe that the second best plane to use is the sharpest plane you have. The best shooting plane is the plane you never have to use. Practice crosscutting precisely to a knife line and you'll spend less time shooting and, more importantly, less time sharpening planes for shooting.

Planes seem to get all the love from hobby woodworkers but it is with chisels that my work gets done. Without my beloved bits of razor sharp steel on wood handles, I would be lost and totally useless in a woodshop. Aside from my full set of Gabriel hollows and rounds, they are most prized tools and the things I would run into a burning shop to save.

One of my favorite chisels by William Butcher

An inexplicably contentious topic is that of the saw nib. The nib, if you don't know, is a tiny metal protuberance that projects vertically from the end on high quality saws made long ago and on some boutique saws made today. There are many theories about the nib, including that it was used to test the temper of the plate, that it was used as a convenient way to tie on a tooth guard to protect the saw, that it was used to score a line on wood to be cut, or that it offered a visual clue to the sawyer when the saw was about to come out of the kerf. I find none of those so-called 'utility nib' theories to be compelling.

Here's my totally untrue story on the creation of the nib...

Everyone knows that woodworkers are slow to complete projects. This is a huge problem when you are working for a living, especially when you are working for someone else, and even more so when you have a date with a lusty serving wench at the local tavern. So, a mid-17th century Dutch-German carpenter, I.M Van Der Fulypunktual, decided that he needed a better way to tell how long he had been at work.

Now, back then, clocks were extremely expensive. All the gears were hand-filed from extremely pricey materials. I.M didn't have enough cash to buy a real clock AND pay for his bier, so he solved the problem in an ingenious manner. He built a portable sundial and riveted in right on the end of his favorite saw. This was perfect for him. He could saw his heart out and know exactly what time it was. But far more importantly, he knew exactly when quitting time was, and when bier-o'clock came around on that sundial, he could quit right away.

Now, the other carpenters in the area were frustrated that I.M. got the best table, the freshest pour and the freshest serving girls at the tavern, so they soon replicated his successful design on their own saws. Soon the entire guild of carpenters were seen as do-nothing drunkards, all thanks to that sundial, which lives on today in the form of the saw nib. Need proof? Just offer a carpenter a cold one...

My real personal theory is that it is the vestigial remnant of a long out of favor saw decoration. The Dutch often decorated their saws with curlicues on the tip of their handsaws. I believe the nib is just the continuation of that decoration. I have tried nearly all of the theories and none of them make sense to me. You may disagree. Outstanding, I'm all for different opinions that are based on facts, not that there are any facts when it comes to the nib. I just don't want to talk about it anymore. No one still living knows why, assuming anyone ever did know for sure.

My most prized possession: a full set of Gabriel hollows and rounds

I believe in pursuing safety in the woodshop. This is one reason I like hand saws instead of table saws. You have to really try to cut your finger off with a handsaw, not so much with the table saw. Handsaws can bite you, of course... that fact that you can count the TPI in an inch-long slice along my right pointer finger is a clear reminder of that. But the finger is still in place and that's the point.

Chisels are the most dangerous tool in a hand tool woodshop. You can quickly and efficiently amputate a digit with a sharp chisel and a mallet. I tried it once. I don't recommend that you do the same. I almost lost the tip of my left pinky finger to a chisel, and my own ignorant ego, when I thought I could balance a too-small blank of wood on end to split out a peg. I was wrong and stuck the thing in right at the fingertip joint. Very lucky to still have it. Chisels are the most dangerous shop tool in my opinion. If I could do my work without chisels I would seriously consider it but it would be an impossible task.

A common category of injuries that happen in the woodshop are stress injuries such as tennis elbow such as planing. Avoiding them takes a multi-pronged approach. Working at a bench of the correct height for your style of work and size makes a big difference in the functional mechanics of how you use your plane. Another is the grip with which you hold your planes. If you have a death grip on the tote, you are likely to be over-tensing the muscles around your elbow, leading to problems like you have described. This is similar to a leading cause of tennis elbow in recreational tennis players, gripping the racquet too tightly. This also happens in military pilots, I have been told. Using improperly sized gloves can lead to over gripping and, in turn, tennis elbow.

The most important safety tip I can give you is this. If you are tired, mad, or otherwise not fully present for your work, turn off the lights, leave the shop, and go do something else. If you rush your work and try to push through these barriers, you will end up hurting yourself or making an unrecoverable mistake. It isn't worth it, especially if you are out for the enjoyment of the craft.

In my opinion, making your own tools is one of the most enjoyable parts of the craft. Anybody can buy a tool and 'own' it but I say that a tool isn't really yours unless you've made it or at least restored it. And it truly becomes yours the day you complete your first project with it... or when you first bleed on it.

Shop-made tools

Closeup of dovetail markers

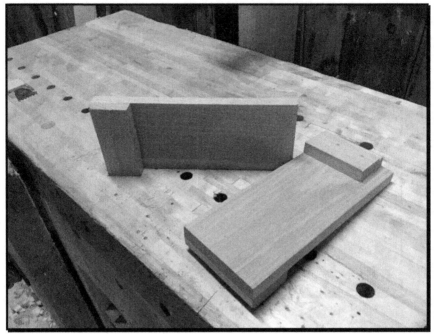

The deceptively simple bench hook

The glorious thing about woodworking tools is that it is often the simplest things that make the most difference in shop practice. Take, for example, the irreplaceable winding sticks. The simplicity of winding sticks is not representative of their importance in the hand tool shop. I think making a pair is a great exercise, and making them a bit fancy is just fine. It is impossible to prepare stock by hand without something to use in this fashion and you might as well make them beautiful. My own pair is made from walnut, the back stick has a piece of extremely curly maple inlaid into it to provide contrast. That said, a pair of commercial levels from the hardware store will work, as will a couple of lengths of aluminum angle.

Another simplistic yet sophisticated tool is the bench hook. The force of gravity and the force of using the tool up against a solid fence is all that it takes to keep the work from moving.

Bench hooks, from the user's perspective

When I made my current bench, I spent a lot of time drilling bench dog holes because that was the thing to do. As I grew in experience, my work holding evolved to the point that they are almost wholly superfluous except as convenient places to stick holdfasts. I have no end vise and see no reason to have one. I have a toothed metal planing stop (installed when I first made the bench), a leg vise, bench hooks, sticking boards, and three holdfasts. My bench has a thick slab top, but I added a wide face board with holdfast holes (a la the Hay Shop benches) that fits my needs perfectly (no bench slave required).

Tools are such an important part of life, not just woodworking but in general. We sweat on them, we bleed on them, we curse them, we owe our progress to them. With respect to Homer Simpson who I shall now paraphrase... to tools, the cause of and solution to all of my woodworking problems.

Making moldings

Vintage miter jack

I never lend tools. The way I see it, if I like someone enough to lend them one of my hand tools, then I might as well give them what they need and help push them down the slope to self-sufficiency and woodworking. So I have a small stash of giveaway tools and they are handed off with the intention of never getting them back. But, if you go anywhere near my "user tools" in my tool chests, we will have words. Just ask my wife... she almost became my ex-wife after I caught her using a Wenzloff half-back to cut back a lilac bush...

Without a doubt, the most important tools you will use in the shop are connected to your body. With a little experience, your hands will become capable of feeling when a surface isn't flat. If you've got good eyesight, you should be able to detect minute variations from square or in twist just by looking at the surface, and with even greater precision when combined with winding sticks. Finally, your brain will help you recognize what work must be done to successfully execute the design.

Much like clamps, the formula for calculating the number of marking gauges you need will always be MG=N+1, where N is the number you have. You'll always realize that you need a different setting on a gauge halfway into a project and it is typically bad practice to reset a gauge you've used on the piece so far until you are absolutely sure you won't need that same measurement again. So, when you find marking or mortising gauges, buy them.

I have a mortising gauge that is pre-set with the width of my favorite mortise chisel. This makes it very easy to set to a given width, unlike the adjustable gauges where the second pin slides around constantly while the fence is adjusted.

Sawing a dado by hand with a guide

18th century molding plane by Madox

ON PROCESS

An Ode to English Pattern Dovetails

I like fat tails and I cannot lie
You other joiners can't deny
When a tail slides in by a little tiny pin
Your joints get sprung

Carvings on display in the Anthony Hay Shop

Trying hard, yet failing, is the first step to success. If there is technique that has stopped you from building something, go after that technique with everything you have. Read books. Send an expert an email asking for guidance. Most importantly, go into the shop and try it. Living in fear of a technique or assuming you aren't 'good enough' at it is a sure way to stunt your growth as a craftsman. I have more respect for the man who tries, fails and shares that failure with the rest of us than I do for the man who tries nothing yet knows all...

In this business, as in life, you pay your money and you take your shot. Sometimes your shot strikes home and you build something amazing, sometime all you produce is firewood. Both are equally important to your long term development as a craftsman, as a designer, and as a human. Don't sell yourself short.

Closeup of chest joinery

Organization is the key to success in any shop. Even if you don't follow a cut list or a measured drawing, knowing what you are going to do before you do it removes a major barrier to success, namely the human mind's tendency to second guess everything. Make a plan, work the plan, complete the plan. Never allow laziness, lack of mental clarity, or a short attention span to trick you into making changes on the fly. Whenever I have done so in my shop I have regretted the decision.

If you ever find yourself stuck on what to do next or how to complete a task in your shop, try asking yourself WWGED? (What Would George Ellis Do). I have often resorted to this technique and it has yet to let me down.

I once tried asking myself WWRUD? (What Would Roy Underhill Do?) but I ended up passing out from the resultant lack of blood.

A gooseneck hanging cabinet with compass rose inlay

When I was younger I used to rant and rave, swear, cuss, and sometimes throw tools in my shop when things didn't work out exactly as I planned. I quickly learned that breaking an expensive tool in an immature fit of rage just made me more angry. Now I just cuss and grab another piece of lumber from the rack. Unless of course I want an excuse to buy a new tool...

Total efficiency in all work processes and methods is an unobtainable, yet still worthy, goal to strive for. Arrange your tools so that what you use most is easy to access. Keep your marking tools at the bench. Don't make eight passes with a hand plane with a fine set when two passes with a coarsely-set plane will do. Use a hatchet, not a saw, to trim an inch in width from a board. The less efficient you are the harder you have to work, which sounds painful and unnecessary in what is supposed to be a fun endeavor. Work smart, not hard, as they say, but the best solution is to not work at all if you don't have to.

Periodically, you should reevaluate what you do and how you do it. Don't fall into the trap of doing things the same way you always did if the only justification is that it is how you've always done it. I recently tried a Japanese plane for the first time and, while I don't see owning any in the near future, it was interesting to get a feel for the process that other people use.

In power tool woodworking, it is very easy to run the board through a powered planer to achieve accurate thickness without breaking a sweat. When working by hand, however, you have to ask yourself about the importance of achieving some nominal thickness for every single board in a project. It isn't always necessary to thickness your board to a fixed dimension or even to flatten the opposite side of the workpiece. Given that it often doesn't matter exactly how thick the board is since each board in a project is cut to fit its mating board, you can get away with simply planing the board to its greatest common thickness.

Many modern woodworkers seek objective perfection without regard for time or effort but then express frustration with how "slow" hand tools are. I readily admit they are slow when using them to achieve that perfection, but this is an inappropriate use of the technology because the user's mind is not calibrated to pre-power tool ways. It may be due to the consideration that for many people, the process is actually the goal, not the product. When the journey is the destination, it is easy to focus on the details along the way, to allow the pursuit of perfection to become the priority and force the goal of a finished piece of furniture into an also-ran.

When preparing lumber by hand, it is very time consuming to achieve an absolutely flat, completely square surface that is parallel with the opposing surface at some exact thickness. This is usually an unnecessary use of your time if you become familiar with the concept of reference surfaces. A reference surface is simply a face or edge (you need one of each) that you focus your time and effort on. You need to rely on those surfaces being flat, straight, and square to each other. It is important that you mark those edges with a pencil once they are completed and that you ensure that those surfaces are the only ones from which you take measurements or lay out cuts or joinery. The success of your project depends on your ability to make and use your reference surfaces correctly.

Planing white oak

I'm an ambidextrous woodworker, meaning that I saw left handed but use planes right handed. I feel equally comfortable using chisels with either hand. I've often wondered if there were any others like me but have never met one. I guess that is one thing that makes me unique. Just like everyone else.

Pine shavings

My technique for rough sawing, whether ripping or crosscutting, relies on keeping my head and most importantly my left eye directly over the cut as much as possible. Please note that I saw left handed so, if you are a righty, keep your right eye over the cut. Keeping the cut properly oriented is easiest this way. To enable this orientation, I use a low saw bench to support the lumber and I hold it in place using my knees and body weight. You should periodically check your saw against the square as you proceed. Use as much of the saw as possible. For crosscuts, I keep the saw angled about 45 degrees from vertical; rip cuts I use about 30 degrees from vertical to make quick progress in the cut. Should the saw drift off the line, drop this angle to 70 or so degrees from vertical; this enables you to use more of the length of the saw plate to regain your straight line. Worry more about cutting to the line than about the speed of your progress.

As you gain experience, your speed, accuracy, and confidence will improve. This is true of many things in life, not just sawing.

Rip sawing white oak

The only "bad" woodworking is the woodworking that doesn't get done, or that which is done without enjoyment. If you aren't being paid to do the job but aren't having fun, why do it at all? I recommend that you take whatever steps are necessary to make the work fun and to make your workspace an enjoyable place to be. If that means buying something new, buy it. If you have to spend a few days deep cleaning your shop, do it. If you get halfway into a project and aren't enjoying yourself, burn it. Move on and find something better to do with your time. I suggest sharpening your tools when this happens and then diving right back in with another project that you find interesting. If you give yourself time off you may not go back.

Making new "antiques" is the type of work I truly enjoy. I love telling stories with the surfaces of the furniture I make. This is why I find most new-looking furniture so boring to look at. Sure, it is shiny and pretty, but where is the heart? I want to see what it will look like after 200 years, having been loved by seven generations. Unfortunately, I probably won't live to see that, so I have no problem helping the process along, in a socially responsible and non-fraudulent manner.

This may sound strange but, as I'm building a piece and especially as I'm finishing it, I like to make up the story of the piece as I go. The furniture itself is a MacGuffin for the story in my head. It is the object around which the story revolves. In this way, I've made furniture for European kings, businessmen from British North America, and a dresser for my adult daughter Abigail (who is about to turn two as I write this).

One must be very careful when doing this, for obvious reasons. When you work with authentic tools in authentic ways and with old lumber, the line between good intentions and outright forgery is extremely narrow. To this end, I always sign a drawer bottom or two in chalk, as was common practice, but I also stamp my name deeply in several hidden places, usually inside the case and once or twice on the case bottom. The last thing in the world I want is for someone to take a piece I've made and call it an antique in ten or twenty years.

A "new antique" chest

**My most famous piece, the William and Mary spice chest from
Popular Woodworking**

I find it nearly impossible to work in a space which is cluttered or otherwise dirty. Unlike many of my fellow galoots, I require a spotless, absolutely clear bench and I always put my tools away properly before calling it a day. The idea of working in a cluttered shop makes my skin crawl. I cannot be productive if I'm tripping over refuse or having to move junk to access my tools.

The irony of this is that my writing desk is hopelessly untidy. I'm not sure what that says about me or my work.

If you think you're not making mistakes, you're not paying attention.

A curly maple desk

Just about the time you think you've mastered something is when you'll make a tremendous, irrecoverable mistake that costs real money or allows a significant amount of your blood to spill onto the work, the bench, or in really severe cases the floor.

Most mastery can be recognized as an illusion if you think about it long enough. At any point when you are working, perhaps even while doing something you've done successfully a thousand times in the past, mistakes can and will bite you. In an uncertain universe, where entropy exists and largely runs the show, your mastery means next to nothing without your focus.

In short, don't get cocky without plenty of bandages on hand and a few extra pieces of wood so you can recreate the piece of wood you just ruined.

Please don't freak out about dovetails. More ink has been spilled talking about dovetail joints than just about any other woodworking topic. To some they are seen as the Alpha and Omega of fine furniture. To others, myself included, they are simply a very useful way to join two boards at a right angle in a strong, long lasting fashion. By creating the mechanical interlock, the joint will likely stay together even if the glue should fail over time. So, despite my lack of interest in dovetails it is important that any prospective craftsman learn how to execute this joint in a functional and efficient manner.

Again, don't freak out about it. Just give it a rip and see what happens. No need for over-analysis. If they are structurally successful, that is all that counts. And if you aren't happy with the looks, slap some molding on them like they didn in the 18th century, when exposed end grain was considered ugly and great pains were taken to ensure it is never seen in polite company.

Working on half-blind dovetails

Sloppy and gappy 18th century dovetails

I hate dovetailing drawers. It is very high on my list of least favorite things to do in the woodshop. It is precise, fiddly work that requires an immense amount of attention to get right. This is perhaps sacrilege but give me a rabbet and nail drawer, as was common on 17th century furniture, any day of the week.

17th century style dovetails

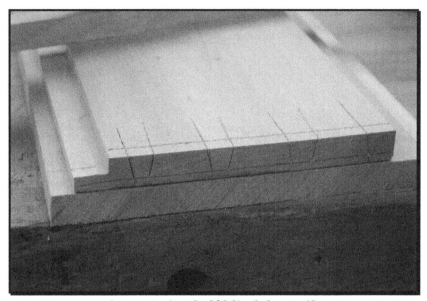

Over-sawing half blind dovetails

One method for transferring dovetail layout

Making stuff from wood is sort of macabre if you think about it. We are making things we put in our homes, furniture, eating utensils, even toys for our children, from the amputated body parts of a once living thing which has been brutally murdered with an ax or a chainsaw. Even as we use it, the personalities and quirks of the original owner come through and force us to adapt. I consider stubborn grain and tearout to be the tree's final revenge.

Everyone complains about the high cost of lumber but no one seems to be willing to sacrifice a virgin to make walnut trees grow faster.

Groovin', possibly on a Sunday afternoon

I am often asked where I get the ideas for the pieces I reproduce. I am most inspired after visiting art museums, furniture collections, and even high-end antique stores and auction houses. Many museums have digitized their collections and they are incredibly valuable resources. The Metropolitan Museum of Art in New York City is, in my opinion, the leader in this area. Auction catalogues and databases are another excellent resource.

Perfection is usually relative. One person's great success is another's total failure. The key is to learn how not to make the same mistake twice or, at least, to learn how to best hide the results.

I believe that the pursuit of perfection in furniture is an outgrowth of our own lack of perfection. We are human and are by definition fallible. We seek to imbue an inanimate object with that which we lack ourselves.

A window sash joint

Carving a gooseneck molding by hand

Replicating a piece of furniture means more than just copying shapes from a photograph and putting on a mirror-like finish. Workmen of the past did not engage in their craft as a worthwhile and enjoyable hobby as most do today; they were simply trying to earn a living so that they might feed themselves, their families, and perhaps save a little for the future. This led them to work quickly and to a salable level. I try to accomplish the same thing in my shop. This often means violating today's aesthetic sensibilities and leaving things behind that show the process. Why this isn't acceptable in modern work I'll never understand. When we work to a pre-industrial standard we free ourselves from the modern idea of perfection and we can gain a bit of appreciation for what it must have been like for the craftsman who came before. I often say I consider myself an experimental archaeologist more than a furniture maker.

Period furniture, even the best examples, exhibits a "Pointilist" quality to my eye. Like impressionist Georges-Pierre Seurat, the craftsmen of the past knew how to combine seemingly crude cuts and shapes into a form that looks very sophisticated when viewed from a distant viewpoint. As with "A Sunday on La Grande Jatte", it's only when you get up close that you begin to understand the technique of the artist at work. Instead of points (a la Seurat), period furniture makers, as a function of their drive to survive, have the gouge marks, layout lines, tearout and joinery gaps (all things we call flaws today) to perfect the composition of the work. Even if we don't notice the "flaws" from a distance, they combine with the overall form and design of the work to produce an obviously handmade and perfectly imperfect piece of furniture.

When moldings are uniform from one end to the next, when your joinery is millimeter-perfect, when your show surfaces look more like plastic than real wood, then we have gone too far when seeking to recreate the furniture of the past. I'm a huge car guy and when a classic car is painted improperly, over detailed and covered in chrome, we call that an "over-restoration". In the same way, I think most modern period furniture is "over-reproduced".

Like most woodworkers I have started far more projects than I have finished. I plan to return to some of them, others are likely just gone forever. Having a bonfire fueled with the bones of dead passions is a powerful way to remind yourself that life is all too short. It's also a great way to make space in the shop for more projects you'll never finish... it's the circle of life of woodworking.

Reading books is no substitute for examining actual furniture, shops, and studying techniques with craftsmen at work and qualified teachers. Do this whenever possible. The best way to learn is to study the old pieces and attempt to replicate the tool marks that you see. Really understand why things look the way they do. Eventually, you will have epiphanies, some minor, some major, that will fundamentally alter the way you work. It's what happened, and is still happening every day, to me. Sometimes a left-over gauge mark isn't a mistake; sometimes a saw overcut is intentional and not a flaw.

I'm a product oriented guy. I don't get hung up with cutting dovetails or about having a chisel that is honed to 15,000 grit and will shave your eyeballs with just a slight look in the direction of the cutting edge. But, I do get a little sentimental about the simple, everyday furniture of the past. And I do take great pleasure in reading the posts of other similar-minded folks.

For example, on a recent trip to the East Coast, I visited the Philadelphia Museum of Art. Of course, I was impressed with the large scale, high end casework, tall clocks, etc., but what really got me were the simple objects. The painted chests that still bore the date of a past marriage. The pine chest of drawers with the turned ball feet in front, one of which had a very prominent, unrepaired shrinkage crack.

These pieces witnessed it all and survive to tell the tale. The dings and scratches that come with real age makes it easy to imagine the historical setting in which the past owners of these pieces lived and died. This is something I find next to impossible with the "tour de force" pieces applauded by antique dealers and reproduced ad nauseum by woodworkers. Many have an air of sterility about them, as if they have never lived outside of a museum setting.

The study of high-end furniture is an interesting work area for some woodworkers. But for me, with rare exception, I'm usually more interested in the simple pieces, things I might have owned had I been born in the 1680s rather than the 1980s. I'm sure I'm not the only person who feels this way. Or maybe I am... but I'm OK with that.

Simple decorative techniques on a pine chest of drawers

Creating a template in pine

Making a tongued board

Do what you can, and just like about 99% of things in woodworking, if it looks right it is right.

ON PEOPLE

"These forgotten people are my fellows. They are the silent ones on whose behalf I want to speak... They left behind visible and tangible objects created by their own hands: dumb things that speak to me across the centuries in a language that no text can reproduce... I feel an affinity with the makers of these things."

- British author Stephen Batchelor

Why do we make things? Why do we put our minds and bodies through the rigors of building furniture when allegedly functional pieces can be purchased for comparatively little from any number of sources? Why do we spend hundreds and perhaps thousands of dollars on tools, wood, glue, and finishes to create something that can be had for 1/10 the cost?

Only you can answer that question for yourself but, since you are reading this book, I suspect you already have a good answer. We just need to share our answers with those who don't understand and push the scourge of sub-par furniture back to the depths of Hell from whence it came.

I am always intrigued at the parallels that can be drawn between humans and woodworking. For example, the process of riving. To rive, you take a rough piece of wood and judiciously apply a tool called a froe to split off the waste wood. The process, when done properly, yields a smaller but stronger piece of wood from which any number of useful things can be made. A human is a bit like that initial rough piece of wood. We are loaded with negative desires and harmful emotions, things that inhibit us from being strong, well-adjusted people. Through judicious application of our most powerful tool, introspection, we can split off some of the waste and end up a stronger person that is more useful to humanity.

My other favorite example of this is the concept of planing. We use a somewhat flat tool to impart near flatness to an otherwise imperfect and constantly moving material. Flatness is a relative goal in most cases. The same can be said of those around us. Humanity itself acts as the plane, trying to enforce morality and societal norms, flattening out what is otherwise a less-than-flat human being into something that fits the straightedge test of society.

The metaphor can be extended to the operational categories of planes. The longer the plane, the straighter a surface you can produce, at least theoretically. I think of the big societal norms, such family, school, religion, and work, as the jointer plane of society. Those things take down the big humps in a subtle fashion. The shorter planes of society, things like popular culture, friends, work, smooth the smaller areas but, like their woodworking equivalents, can't efficiently accomplish the goal on their own. Humans, like wood, can be rough, can be twisted, can force you to work against the grain, and can resist any attempt at regulation.

We work wood by hand to make a natural material into something artificial. Maybe in doing so we trade some of our own artificiality and trade it for a whisper of the natural essence that was once in the tree. Maybe that is why we do what we do, we seek a connection with nature that we have lost over time.

Shavings from a molding plane

The echo chamber of the woodworking media, including online fora, is strong. Truths and non-truths reverberate with equal frequency and, unfortunately, the same validity. Escape! Think for yourself! Try things! Think about things! Make mistakes! Make discoveries!

The work that period woodworkers were able to accomplish with such a small kit is astonishing, when you compare it with the level of tooling present in most modern shops, even hobby shops. I tend to agree with Adam Cherubini on this point: he's mentioned that most woodworkers are equipped in a fashion more similar to a 1900s production shop than that of an 18th century woodshop, but that most of our woodworking output is geared more to a 18th century shop mindset (smaller volume, one-off pieces not production runs).

One thing that contributed to the output of period woodworkers and their small kits is the level of specialization. For example, in many cases they bought wood already sawn to the proper size and thickness by professional sawyers, eliminating the need for rough hewing / planing / sawing. A Philadelphia chairmaker probably wouldn't have needed carving chisels, as he would have had a professional carver do that portion of the work. He likely wouldn't have finished his own chair, as there were professional finishers to do that job. Upholstery was the same deal. In contrast, modern woodworkers do it all, and most of us are self-trained, unlike period woodworkers who would likely have had at least a minimal apprenticeship with a skilled master.

Modern woodworkers are frequently doing the work of several skilled craftsman with significantly less training that the average worker of the past. Because of this, the projects that modern woodworkers complete on a regular basis are just as impressive, if not more so, than the 18th century pieces we all revere. It also, in some ways, explains the woodworking community and its obsession with tools, as we are all fighting an uphill battle against basic human nature. We can't do everything or be good at everything, so we all seek the next great thing to allow us to cut those perfect dovetails, or carve the Newport shell, or apply a French polish in 20 minutes. It's a losing battle, but one that makes a great deal of money for some people.

Like a lot of guys, I'm just trying to get off the merry-go-round, be happy with the tools I have and can find / restore, and make the best furniture and sash that I can with what skills I've got.

Once you develop an eye for design, it can absolutely ruin your life. You'll obsess over the most minor proportion errors, material selections, or poor line choices. I was kicked out of the only Ikea store I have ever dared set foot in for loudly criticizing the 'termite barf' with which their alleged "furniture" was produced.

A few planes from a toolchest I purchased

Just about anyone who says they aren't screwing something up, on some level, on a daily basis, either isn't paying close enough attention, doesn't actually understand their error, or is simply lying to cover it up. Absolute perfection is impossible because we are all, theoretically at least, human. Making an error once is normal human behavior. It is in making the mistake repeatedly that one begins to learn why the mistake is being made and, with proper reflection sometimes teaching, the person can learn how not to repeat the mistake.

The best artisans in the world are the ones who have made thousands and thousands of mistakes but have learned how not to make them time after time. They progress and they learn to make different and higher-level mistakes, mistakes that they see that guys who are still stuck on the easier mistakes may not see or understand because they aren't there yet.

Being an outstanding craftsman doesn't mean you can teach someone else to be a fine worker. Being a good teacher doesn't necessarily mean you are an outstanding craftsman.

In short, mistakes are the true teachers. The best way to learn is by making them yourself. The next best way is to have an outstanding craftsman share his mistaking making experience. Having a good teacher tell you what they know can be useful, but without the first-hand screw-up factor, I'd place it third in the hierarchy of potential for learning.

Planing stock with a wooden bench plane

Woodworker's Block is all too real. I absolutely suffer from this from time to time.. There are times when it turns my stomach to even think about going into the shop because I leave so much of myself there when working, both physically and mentally.. I sometimes take a sabbatical from the shop for a few months or more. After I finished writing my first book, it took me a year to rekindle the fire needed to work in the woodshop. So I restored cars instead. My point in telling you this is that any creative or technical work, even if it isn't in the woodshop proper, helps you build your skills, develop your designer's eye, and makes you a better woodworker in the end. If you ever get stuck, follow this sage advice: "If you have no design sense, copy a good design instead of making bad designs.".

I find the study of what inspires woodworkers to be fascinating. Some woodworkers spend their entire lives obsessed with recreating a certain style, using one particular material, or with executing one particular detail or decorative technique with perfection. It is akin to what some fine artists do. For example, Picasso painted in nearly monochromatic blue / green for three years. Jackson Pollock made his famous splatter paintings for the better part of his career, though he started out as a Regionalist under Thomas Hart Benton. And Gauguin sure loved Tahiti.

And yet, for every woodworker obsessed with one thing, there are many others bounce from subject to subject, picking different subjects or even designing their own. I wish I could be like them and escape my near manic obsession with William and Mary furniture. Every time I try to design something of my own it ends up looking like something Marot would have penned. It can be very frustrating at times,

A hanging tool chest

It's funny, despite the fact that I often share information online, I still prefer a good old fashioned print magazine. And print books. And print newspapers. I really don't like the paradigm which we are shifting towards. I'd like to think the whole e-woodworking thing will run its course soon. I just hope the good magazines, namely Popular Woodworking and Fine Woodworking, will survive in a form that still works for me, my needs, and my interests.

The new print magazine fresh in the mailbox and the smell of a book fresh from the printer has an excitement factor that a little blue link in an email cannot match. Maybe I'm just a Luddite at heart.

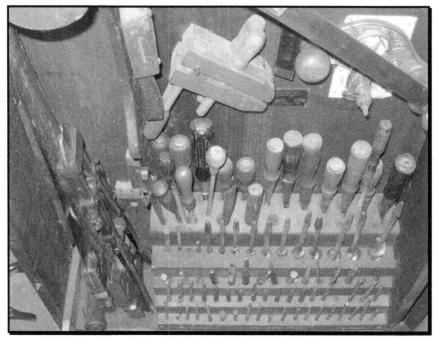

Contents of a toolbox in my collection

One common question I am often asked is why hand tools are experiencing their current renaissance. Hand tool woodworking is exploding today because there are a large number of people frustrated with technology. Many of us spend eight, ten, twelve hours in front of a screen every day and function more as a computer system component than a human being.

In Abraham Maslow's 1943 hierarchy of human needs, he lists near the top of that pyramid the idea of self-actualization, meaning that a person must become what he or she can become, achieve what they can, strive for the highest possibility, in order to be a whole human being. When we get trapped in a computer, we may not be achieving all that we can. The human species is a species of builders, always has been and likely always will be. Hand tools allow us to execute that drive without plugging into a computer system or becoming yet another cog in a larger system.

But Maslow also included the concept of belonging. The internet community has obviously been a huge part of the resurgence in hand tool woodworking. We hand tool guys tend to be historically isolated people. In the old days, apprentices were expected to keep the secrets of the craft and in the more recent past, we've been the "weird guys." We talk about citric acid rust removal for a molding plane iron rather than just buying a new router bit. We're the ones who would actually try to resharpen our own handsaws instead of just running down to the hardware for a new table saw blade. We like it when our projects actually look like they were made by a human, rather than having robot-like machined surfaces. An online community that reinforces that it is ok to be beyond the Norm, to steal Roy Underhill's phrase, is a fantastic thing.

Elaborate handle on a tool chest I own

In addition to the psychological reasons, there are simply practical reasons as well. Many people are living in smaller houses, apartments, and on tighter budgets. This means that the money, floor space, and nearby neighbors (precluding loud power tools) could make woodworking difficult. Hand tools can be less expensive (says the guy with well over 1,000 planes...), quieter, and can be used safely in a much smaller footprint than can power tools.

I prefer to think of the artisans of British North America as being no different than we are. They lived, worked, and died in an uncertain world, just like us. Like us, they faced violence from organized foes who sought to harm them. Like us, they faced the possibility of death by disease outbreak. Like us, they had bills to pay, children to raise, futures to plan for. I think if we look to make generalizations about "simpler times" or "things were slower back then", we miss out on a lot. We rob the people of the past of a large part of their humanity, and we are poorer for it.

Carpenter's Hall in Philadelphia

The original fireplace and chimney from the joinery at
Monticello

A crown molding plane made by Roy Underhill

Rack of planes made by Clark & Williams (now Old Street Tool)

I have spent the better part of the last five years obsessed with walnut William and Mary furniture. The period between about 1690 and about 1720, in America, anyway, produced some of the most beautiful pieces of furniture in the history of the art. From the staggering heights of a high chest to a simple book stand, William and Mary has something for everyone, yet is all too often ignored.

My love for the style has a deep source. For when I see William and Mary furniture, I don't just see walnut and brass shaped in a pleasing fashion. I see the very nature of world history itself. I am borderline obsessed, in the literal and clinical meaning, with world history. The history of the world is encoded in the pieces made during this time. The William and Mary style we know today found its way to the American colonies after it became popular in England following the Glorious Revolution of 1688. William of Orange, Stadtholder of the United Provinces of the Netherlands, became King which highlights the nature of the laws of succession in Europe and the wars they brought about. He brought with him a Huguenot artist and designer named Daniel Marot.

Marot was refugee from the religious oppression rampant in 17th-century France. He brought French design sensibilities, tempered them with the steady and somber nature of Dutch furniture, fired them with a glaze of elements from the Italian Renaissance before ultimately painting them with themes drawn from the Asian influence brought into Europe through the Dutch East India Company. Those designs made their way through English society and, ultimately, to us here in the Colonies. For one who understands the history of Europe, this amalgamation and adaptation is plainly evident in the William and Mary style. Every time I see a William and Mary piece, I'm reminded of the foundations of our modern world. I don't get this sense from any other furniture style.

My love isn't just of the esoteric nature of the style. From a woodworking standpoint, William and Mary pieces offer interesting technical challenges. Cases with legs which are dowelled or otherwise fitted with a round tenon to connect them with a case, extensive use of veneer, japanning, ebony and ebonizing... the list goes on. As much as I appreciate the history those pieces represent, I also appreciate the technical nature of the work.

Here is a snapshot into my path to becoming a professional furniture maker, written for Popular Woodworking, though not printed, in 2012:

> I'll admit it. I used to be one of those shadowy guys you heard about on the news, spinning the truth to

make a point, trading political influence for campaign donations and annoying the public with television ads and phone calls asking for your vote. I was all that is wrong with American politics: I was a professional campaign manager and I was good at my job. It consumed nearly every aspect of my life, but the rewards were immense.

Despite my professed love of battling in the political arena, I had a strong desire to escape that world of half-truths and paper victories. I wanted to do something more meaningful with my life, to create something that stands the test of time, not victories that are forgotten in a year. I wanted to escape the 100 hour work weeks, the constant phone calls from politicians, and the continuous pandering to whoever has the biggest checkbook. Most importantly, I wanted to be a better husband by being at home with my wife instead of being on the road constantly.

I had learned a little about the craft from my family. As a result of this introduction, and my own work in studying books from the masters (Thanks Roy!), I learned to love historical woodworking and carpentry. After a 12 or 14 hour day on the job, I turned to my bench to alleviate stress. Even at 2am, I would retreat to my basement shop to work on a project. When travelling around Michigan from campaign office to campaign office, I would find every antique store along the way and quickly hunt for old tools. My fun distraction turned into a full-blown obsession.

The easy availability of old tools and the necessity to work quietly influenced me to work only with hand tools. To me, old hand tools are more fun to find, and use, than new power tools. Besides, wives tend to get angry when you fire up a universal motor at "dark-thirty" in the morning. Hand tool woodworking gave me the freedom to do what I wanted, when I wanted, and gave me a chance to do something where the only happiness that mattered was my own. I knew that this, not politics, was my future.

By January of 2011, I had had enough. I left politics to start a small woodworking business, making custom furniture and window sash by hand. I've had some successes, and a few setbacks, but I get to make a little money doing what I love. I've been privileged to demonstrate my craft for MWTCA, SAPFM and local craft and self-sufficiency fairs. Thanks to hard work and a little luck, my business is growing. Of course, I couldn't get by without the support, and health insurance, provided by my incredible wife.

This year we are fleeing a small but noisy city, and are buying a large farmhouse in the rural area where we both grew up. I'm building a timber frame building to house my shop and to provide a small classroom space so I can begin to pass some of what I've learned about the craft to others. And one day, after we start our family, I hope to teach my children the most important thing I've learned so far: Work to live, don't live to work.

At some point in your woodworking career you will probably start to think that it would be great to leave whatever work you do for a living and make stuff full time. I'm not going to say it is impossible because it obviously isn't impossible. Many craftsman have managed to do just that. I do think you need to take a long, hard look at who you are, your finances, your goals for your life, and how your outlook on the hobby will change when you turn it into your full time gig. I did exactly that, once upon a time, and didn't make it very long for a variety of reasons. I still sell most of what I make but it isn't my only source of income... and neither is writing about woodworking. I now offer you a group of thoughts to consider before making that big jump.

Why do you work with wood?

Even though you work for "yourself", it is important to remember that you actually work for a large group of other people. You have to meet their deadlines, their design ideas, and their expectations. You have to please people other than just yourself. Escaping that fact is often an important reason why people take up woodworking to begin with; they want to do something for themselves, things that make them happy. When people are paying you to make them happy, what you want goes out the window.

This fact was the largest reason I left full-time woodworking. I grew weary of dealing with the demands of customers who wanted high quality work at Ikea prices. Building things that other people wanted, things that didn't interest me at all or in styles in which I have little to no experience was the fast track to closing up shop. Now, I choose the projects. I get to build whatever I want on speculation and then sell it. If it doesn't sell for a while, fine, I discount it a bit and wait. If it doesn't sell at all, it's no problem. I've made something that I truly love so I can live with it in my own house for as long as it takes.

This goes hand in hand with the fact that I get truly bored with most things after a period of time. I can't imagine cranking out a run of the exact same table or bookcase or building set after set of kitchen cabinets. If I don't like something I don't have to do it. It is an incredible freedom.

How comfortable are you with being broke most of the time?

You may be lucky and establish a booming business of repeat clients with sufficient net worth to make a profit at this business. Some craftsman are able to do this. I think it is important, however, to recognize that this level of clientele takes years to build up. It doesn't happen overnight, if at all, and you probably need to eat, clothe your kids, and keep a roof over your head in the meantime. This might mean you keep your day job a little while longer than you'd like, or perhaps you have a spouse that provides steady income and, ideally, health insurance.

When you're self-employed or trying to become self-employed, remember that cash flow is king. Before making the leap, pay off as much debt as possible. Cut out the expensive luxuries that eat up your bank account. Figure out the pain points with regards to the budget by seeing how little you can actually live on per month. Remember, too, that there are no paid sick days. No paid vacations. No paid training. Everything comes out of your own pocket and if you aren't working you aren't getting paid.

Can you sell yourself and your work without feeling like a total shill?

I think that most of us harken back to *Field of Dreams* and think "If I build it, they will come". That only works in the movies. It takes hard work and an advertising budget of time, money, or both, to get clients to call you. The rise of social media such as Instagram has made it less expensive to get your work in front of the public but, when you work for yourself, every hour of unbillable work you put in becomes extremely expensive. It is important to remember that fact with everything you do.

Marketing myself was always the toughest part of being self-employed. I always prefer to let my work speak for itself but I quickly realized that the work can only speak if someone sees it. Getting people to see it is a big part of the battle. Even today, with a large portfolio of work and after many magazine and journal articles and this, my second book, I have a hard time selling myself as any sort of expert in pre-industrial woodworking. I always feel like a shill. You can't feel that way if you're going to make it.

When I jumped to full-time woodworking I struggled to create answers to many of the questions. That is why I decided that it wasn't for me. I now make things as one of several of my "side hustles" as the young people of today call it. I also write about my woodworking experiences and publish my prose in various formats including the very one you are reading right now. This has proved to be a highly successful way of working for me and my family. I still get to work wood essentially for free, I get to say no to any client or project I don't want to work with, and I have money in the bank. Win - win - win.

It is said that the truly successful are able to chase their dreams without allowing interference from others to get in the way. They don't let the words of those who have failed deter them from finding the way forward. I hope that you are wildly successful if you try to make a go of it. None of my words are intended to stop you from making a career out of working with wood. I just want you to have a realistic picture of what it means.

"Experience is not what happens to a man; it is what a man does with what happens to him." - Aldous Huxley

The source from which the whole craft flows

A workbench hidden away at Monticello

I think it is safe to say that never before in our history have so many woodworkers been able to share their thoughts, their processes, and their projects with the world. The Internet has been a great democratizing force, giving all of us the chance to write whatever we want. If we are good, the Internet can also help us find an audience. I know that my career in writing about woodworking would not exist without the blogging paradigm.

I started my blog, The Eaton County Woodworker, some ten years ago. It gave me a portfolio of work, a body of readers I could point to, and enough gravitas to pitch my first articles to Popular Woodworking Magazine.

I was far from successful at first. I often wrote in a clinical, cold fashion, more like a term paper than a conversation. I still do that sometimes but I'm trying to get better about it. I hope this book showcases those changes to my style. I seem to have found my own voice again.

My shop

My inspiration... the Joiner's Shop at Williamsburg

The timbers that would come together to build my shop

My timber frame shop, mostly raised

Standing in the timber frame (Photo by April Dillinger)

When something goes the way you imagined it would go, don't rest on your laurels. Don't assume that the next time will go as planned. Success breeds success, this is true, but only if you work even harder to make it happen the next time. Each level of success requires double or triple the effort of the previous achievement. This is a lesson I learned a little later in life.

Demonstrating at the Detroit Institute of Arts

I will leave you with one final thought. Showcase your work, no matter if it is 'good enough' or not. Teach others what you've learned, share your experiences with kids and adults alike. Those of us who work with our hands have a duty to future generations. That duty is to show that working with your hands is an honorable, respectable, practical, and most of all enjoyable way to spend the limited time you have on this planet.

Ruined mansions along the James River in Virginia

The author

ABOUT THE AUTHOR

Zachary Dillinger owns and operates The Eaton County Joinery, a period reproduction furniture shop. In addition to his work as a period reproduction furniture maker, he is a USPAP-compliant appraiser of fine and decorative art, specializing in antique furniture and tools, for Wipiak Consulting and Appraisals. He also works as a freelance writer and appraiser for RM Sotheby's.

He has written articles for *Popular Woodworking Magazine, Fine Woodworking Magazine, American Period Furniture* (the journal of the Society of American Period Furniture Makers), *Early American Life Magazine,* and the newly-created *Mortise & Tenon Magazine.* His first book, *With Saw, Plane and Chisel: Making Historic American Furniture with Hand Tools*, was published in December 2016.

His work has been featured at furniture shows and museums around the country. He has demonstrated period techniques for the Society of American Period Furniture Makers, The Furniture Project, L.L. Johnson Lumber Company, and at numerous historical events. His work has been adjudged to be "Museum Quality" by *Early American Life Magazine* and was juried into their exclusive and prestigious Directory of Traditional American Crafts for three consecutive years.

Zachary is a member of the Society of American Period Furniture Makers, the Midwest Tool Collectors Association, and is a Student Affiliate of the Appraisers Association of America. He holds a BA in Political Science from Michigan State University and also studied fine and decorative art appraisal and connoisseurship at New York University. He lives in Michigan with his wife April and their two year old daughter Abigail.

Made in the USA
Las Vegas, NV
27 January 2021